What on Earth Is

Climate Change?

Oliver and David West

Published in 2024 by Enslow Publishing, LLC
2544 Clinton Street
Buffalo, NY 14224

Designed and illustrated by David West

Cataloging-in-Publication Data

Names: West, Oliver. | West, David.
Title: What on Earth is climate change? / by Oliver and David West.
Description: New York : Enslow Publishing, 2024. | Series: What on Earth is... | Includes glossary and index.
Identifiers: ISBN 9781978534315 (pbk.) | ISBN 9781978534322 (library bound) | ISBN 9781978534339 (ebook)
Subjects: LCSH: Climatic changes--Juvenile literature. | Global warming--Juvenile literature. |
Nature--Effect of human beings on--Juvenile literature.
Classification: LCC QC903.15 W478 2024 | DDC 363.738'74--dc23

Printed in the United States of America

CPSIA compliance information: Batch #CSENS24: For further information contact Enslow Publishing LLC 1-800-398-2504.

Find us on

CONTENTS

This is our home,

planet EARTH.

Our home is in a **cosmic balance**

with our **SUN**.

Heat from our Sun keeps our home *warm*.

Some **heat** bounces off, some is trapped by **clouds** and atmospheric **gases**.

There is a **perfect temperature** for our **planet**.

This **perfect temperature**...

...keeps all living things **happy** and **healthy**.

When you go **outside** today, is it **warm** and **sunny**?

Or is it **cold** and **raining**?

You are seeing what the **weather** is like where you are today.

Weather can change many times in one day.

CLIMATE is different from **weather**.

There are five basic climate regions on Earth.

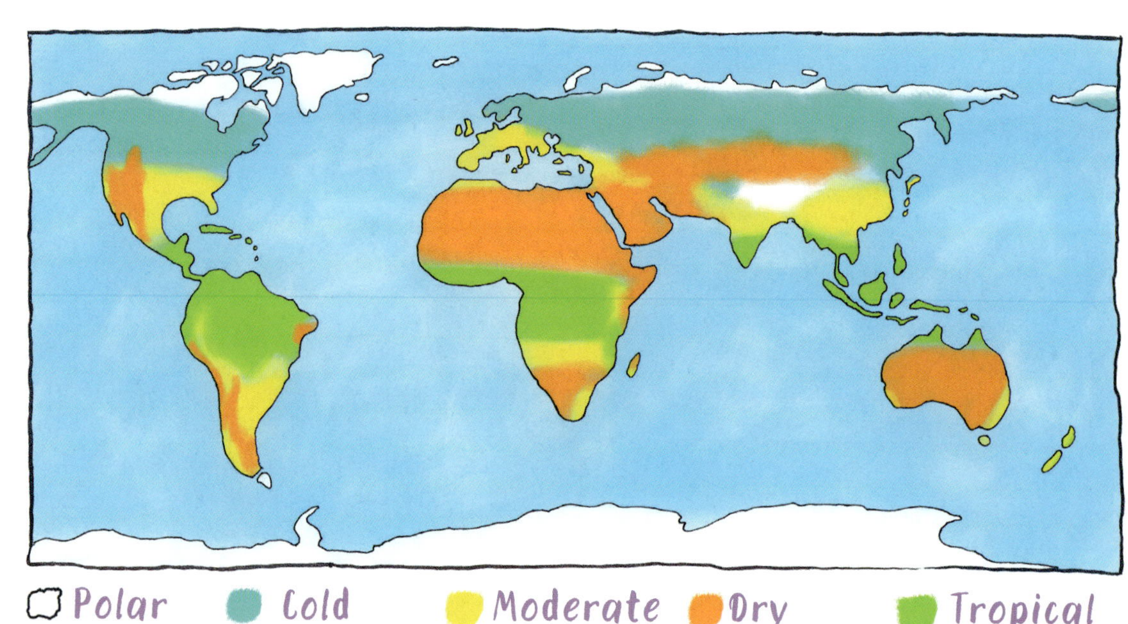

CLIMATE describes **weather** conditions for an entire region for the past **30 years** or more.

When **EARTH's *balance*** is lost, the **CLIMATE** changes.

EARTH's CLIMATE has changed many times before.

There have been much **warmer** times (called **Hothouse Earths**)...

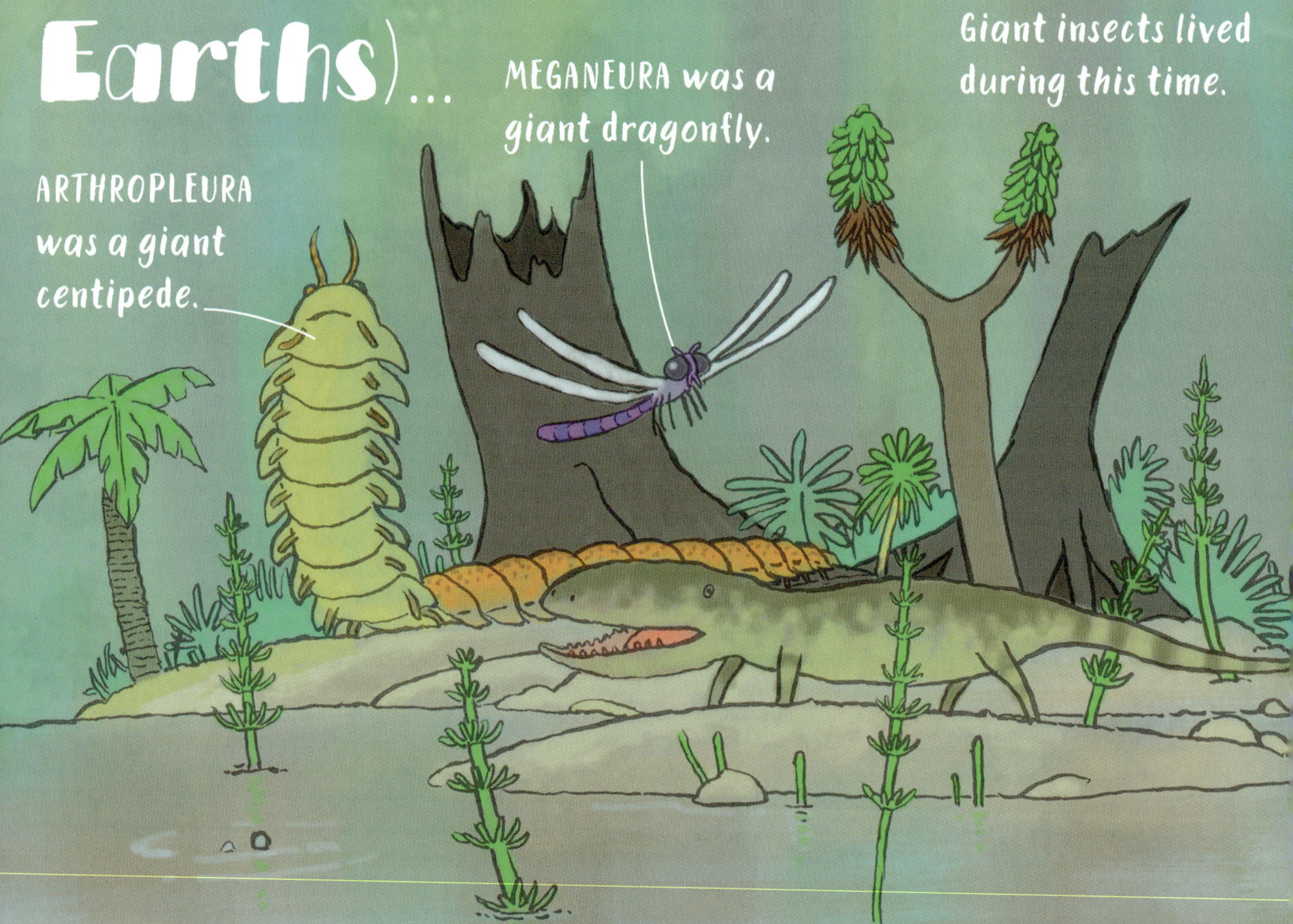

The early CARBONIFEROUS PERIOD (359.2 to 299 million years ago) had a global temperature of 68°Fahrenheit (20°Celsius) compared with 58°F (14.4°C) today.

... and much colder times (called **Icehouse Earths**) when the **Earth** experienced **Ice Ages**.

During the last ICE AGE many mammals grew thick, woolly coats to keep warm.

There have been at least five major ICE AGES. The last began 2.58 million years ago. Average temperatures were 52°F (11.1°C) colder than it is today.

These changes in **EARTH's climate** have **NATURAL CAUSES**, such as...

Earth's orbit has taken it farther from the Sun.

The Sun's energy varies over time.

Earth gets cooler as it gets farther from the Sun.

variations in **EARTH's orbit** and in the **Sun's energy**...

...**volcanic eruptions** caused by **EARTH**'s moving crust...

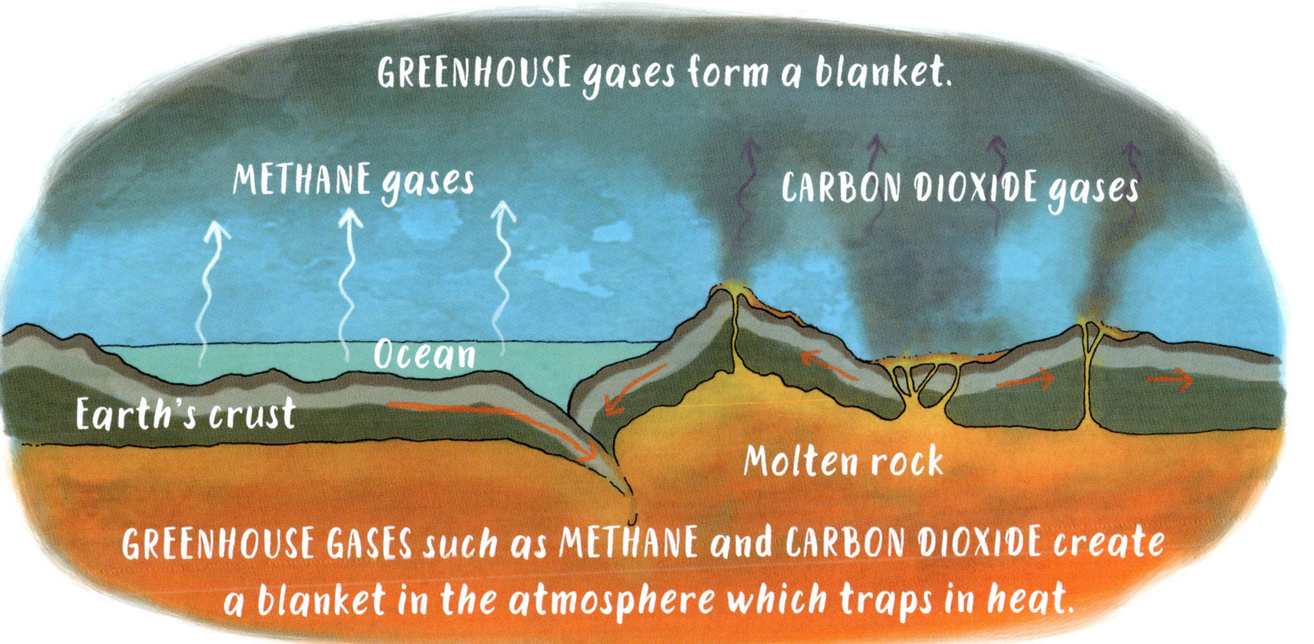

...and trapped **gases released** from the oceans.

Big shifts in climate can have disastrous effects on living things as they **struggle to adapt** to extreme changes.

The DINOSAURS were wiped out 65 million years ago by a BIG SHIFT in Earth's climate after a large METEORITE struck the planet.

The extinction of DINOSAURS
allowed MAMMALS to thrive.

Human activity has increased **GREENHOUSE GASES**, upsetting **EARTH's natural balance**...

...by burning **FOSSIL FUELS**...

...and cutting down FORESTS.

Earth's forests absorb CARBON DIOXIDE from the atmosphere.

Cutting down forests means there is more CARBON DIOXIDE in the atmosphere.

Intensive farming has created problems...

Livestock such as **cattle** release **METHANE** (the most potent **greenhouse gas**).

Buried garbage in **landfill sites** also releases **METHANE** into our atmosphere.

Greenhouse gases keep **EARTH** warm, just like the glass in a **GREENHOUSE**...

...but too much **greenhouse gas** makes **EARTH** overheat...

...leading to **melted ICE CAPS** and **GLACIERS**. This will cause **SEA LEVELS** to rise by more than **220 feet (67 meters)**, **FLOODING** vast areas of low-lying land.

Melting PERMAFROST in cold regions releases more ***greenhouse gases***, speeding up the **GREENHOUSE EFFECT**.

As the PERMAFROST melts, carbon trapped in it is released as CARBON DIOXIDE and METHANE.

SEMI-FROZEN LAYER

PERMAFROST LAYER (made of rock, soil, sand, and ice)

UNFROZEN LAYER

With all the **ICE melted**, less heat from the Sun will be **reflected**, warming **EARTH** even more.

As Earth heats up, WEATHER PATTERNS will change...

What can we do to stop **EARTH** overheating?

We can stop releasing **greenhouse gases** by driving **ELECTRIC VEHICLES**...

...using more RENEWABLE ENERGY...

Renewable energy uses Earth's natural energy from WIND, SUNLIGHT, WATER, AND HEAT FROM THE GROUND.

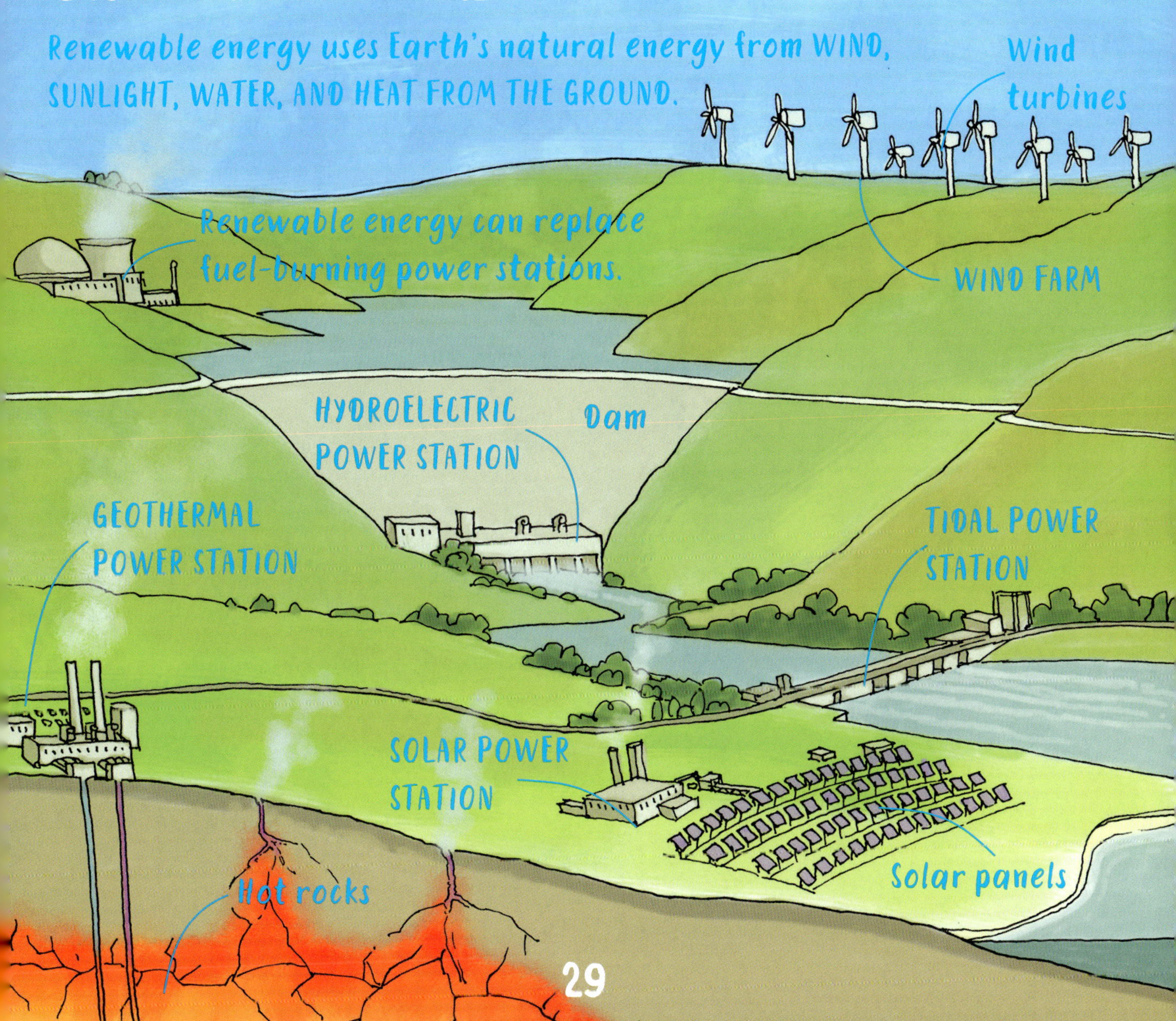

...and even small things like

recycling and **planting trees**

can help...

FOOD WASTE sent to special processing plants can be transformed into fertilizer, instead of producing METHANE in landfill sites.

More trees mean that more CARBON DIOXIDE is locked up.

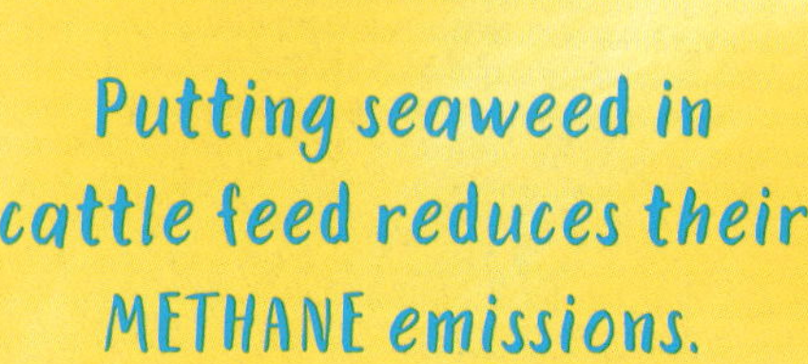

Putting seaweed in cattle feed reduces their METHANE emissions.

...make a happier **EARTH**.

WORDS EXPLAINED

ABSORBED Taken in or soaked up.

ADAPT Change to suit new conditions.

ATMOSPHERE The gases surrounding a planet like Earth.

CARBON DIOXIDE A colorless gas present in Earth's atmosphere that acts as a greenhouse gas.

COSMIC Relating to the universe or cosmos, as it is sometimes called.

EXTINCT No longer in existence.

INTENSIVE FARMING Where a much higher amount of produce is obtained from an area of land.

METEORITE A rock from space that enters Earth's atmosphere.

METHANE A powerful greenhouse gas found in small amounts in Earth's atmosphere.

ORBIT The path of an object such as a planet or spacecraft around a star, planet, or moon.

POTENT Having great power or effect.

THRIVE To develop or grow well.

TROPICAL Having to do with hot and humid areas of the Earth.

INDEX